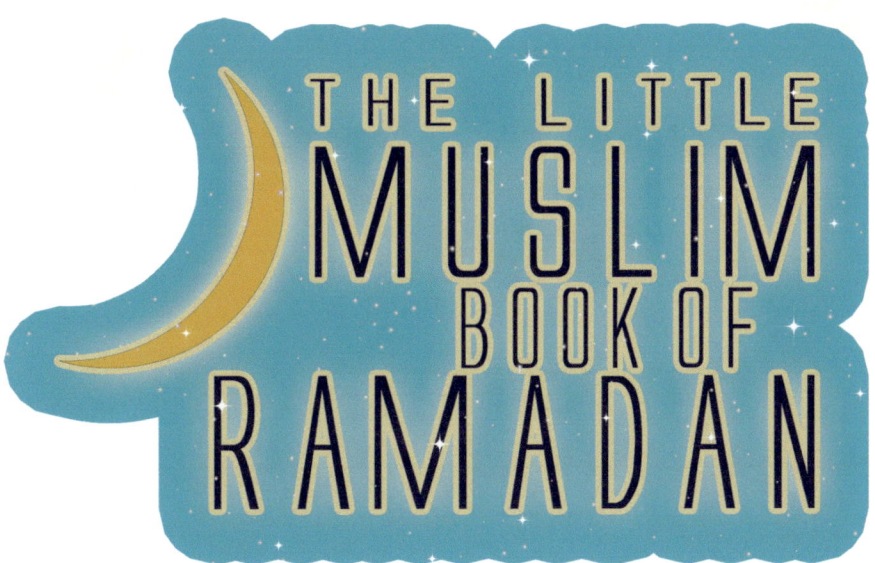

A Green Fig Book

Illustrated & Designed by

CHY Illustration & Design

Name: _____

_____

PUBLISHER: GREEN FIG
PENNSYLVANIA, USA

www.**gogreenfig**.com
info@**gogreenfig**.com

Dear Parents & Educators

The month of Ramadan is the best month of the year. Muslims around the world look forward to witness this blessed month and engage in acts of obedience, such as fasting, praying, remembering the poor and a lot more.

The Little Muslim book of Ramadan explains the fundamental concepts around this month in a style that is easily grasped by youngsters, making it an indispensable fact book for your child's Islamic library and a valuable reference book in classrooms and schools' libraries! Beautifully illustrated by CHY, this book will support parents and teachers to explain what this specific month holds and reinforces the love to the Religion in general. With information about the 'Eid occasion as well, this book serves as a memorable gift and an opportunity to bond with the child on joyful occasions.

We will be happy to hear from you at gogreenfig@gmail.com

Green Fig Team

Ramadan
is the ninth month of the Islamic calendar.

There are 12 lunar months in the Islamic calendar.
Do you know their names?

Muslims wait for Ramadan with excitement and prepare for it with great joy.

During **Ramadan**, the doors of **Paradise** are opened and the doors of **Hellfire** are closed.

Paradise is where the believers will go to in the Hereafter and where they will live happily forever.

Muslims FAST in Ramadan. They don't eat or drink during the day from dawn to sunset.

Muslims have a special meal in Ramadan before dawn which helps them to fast, it is called

as-sahoor.

There is a blessing in as-sahoor, even if it was just a sip of water!

In some countries, a person passes in the streets with a drum to wake people up for Suhoor.

He is called at-tabbal or al-musaharati.

Each day, Muslims break their fast when the day ends at sunset.

Sunset happens when the disc of the sun completely disappears in the western horizon.

It is good to break one's fast right after sunset, and it is Sunnah to do it with dates. If dates are not available, then with water. This meal is called iftār.

Muslims obey God when they fast in Ramadan.

Some of the wisdoms of fasting is to remember the situation of the Hereafter and to give the hungry and the poor money and food.

Muslims do a lot of good deeds in Ramadan. They give a lot of charity. The reward of charity is big.

An example of charity is to give money, food, or clothes to a needy person for God's sake.

Reward is what the believer will get in the Hereafter as a result of his good deeds.

They invite each other for iftār.

They read the
Qur'ān.

The Qur'ān is the best Divine Book. It was revealed to Prophet Muḥammad ﷺ in Arabic.

They gather in mosques to pray tarāweeh.

Tarāweeh is a special sunnah prayer in Ramadan done after the nightfall prayer.

Muslims pray five prayers during the day and night. Do you know all their names?

Dawn Prayer, Noon Prayer, Mid-Afternoon Prayer, Sunset Prayer, Nightfall Prayer.

They wake up at night and make lot of supplication (du'ā').

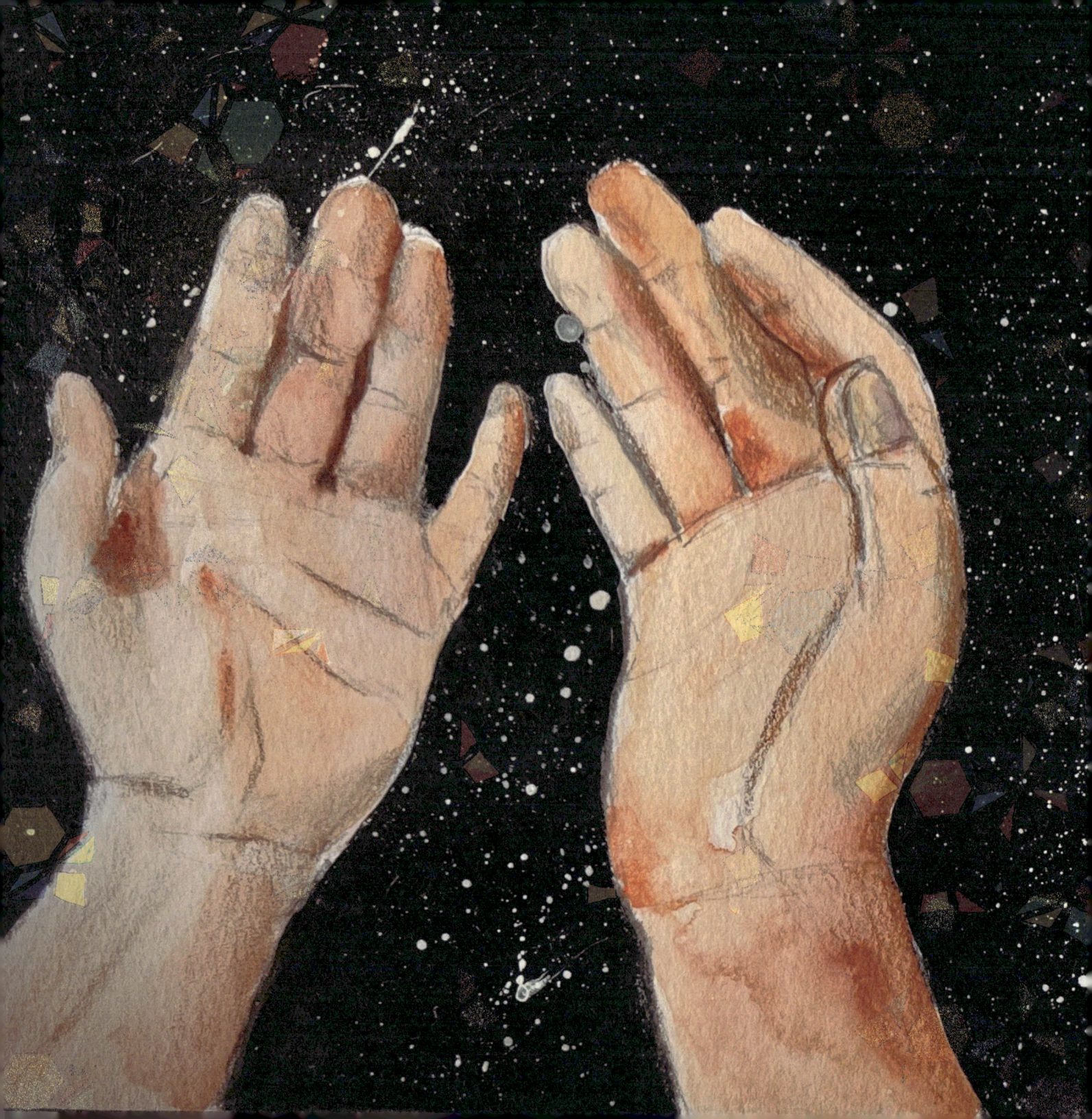

In Ramadan comes the best night of the year. It is called Laylatul-Qadr. It is a special night that Muslims seek to do lot of du'ā' and other good deeds. The reward of good deeds in this blessed night is more than that of one thousand months!

Laylatul-Qadr can be any night of Ramadan; but most of the time, it is one of the last ten nights. During this night, some good people see strong beautiful lights, and some see angels.

Ramadan is either 29 or 30 days like all the other months in the Islamic calendar. After twenty-nine days of Ramadan, Muslims look for the crescent after sunset. If they see it, Ramadan would only be 29 days that year. If not, Muslims fast for 30 days.

When Ramadan ends, 'Eid Al-Fi_tr arrives. Muslims all over the world celebrate this joyous occasion.

In the morning of 'Eid, Muslims pray a special prayer. They congratulate and visit each other. They invite each other to eat together and do a lot of good deeds. Children have so much fun during 'Eid. In many countries, children go to special fair grounds where they get to play and have enjoyable rides.

We love Ramadan, the best month of the year!

CHY Illustration & Design

Yara Mahdi is a passionate artist who has been illustrating GreenFig books since their inception. She is keen on ensuring that every single drawing is uniquely original and reflective of the essence of the book in scope. Together with her father, a professional and talented graphic designer, they established CHY Illustrations and design, the latter which plays a major role in the creative works that GreenFig launches. Yara boosts her talent with her college education in fine arts and is eager on sharing her skills with young talented artists.

Proud Muslim Kids

The Proud Muslim Kids series by Green Fig is designed to engagingly teach youngsters basic concepts of Islam in a way that speaks to their hearts and minds. Each book in the series is crafted by a staff of qualified educators, writers, illustrators, parents and children. Not only is the Proud Muslim Kids series designed to supplement the early childhood and elementary Islamic curriculum, it is a great addition to any school or home library. Covering a wide variety of topics such as the Five Pillars of Islam, Islamic culture, and Islamic history, parents and children will return to these books and enjoy them together time and time again.

Made in the USA
Columbia, SC
15 June 2025